PIERRE BERTON

STEEL ACROSS THE SHIELD

ILLUSTRATIONS BY PAUL MC CUSKER

M&S

An M&S Paperback Original from
McClelland & Stewart Inc.
The Canadian Publishers

An M&S Paperback Original from McClelland & Stewart Inc.

Canadian Cataloguing in Publication Data

Berton, Pierre, 1920-
Steel across the shield

(Adventures in Canadian history. Canada move west)
Includes index.
ISBN 0-7710-1422-8

1. Canadian Pacific Railway Company – History – Juvenile literature.   2. Railroads – Ontario, Northern – History – 19th century – Juvenile literature.   I. McCusker, Paul.   II. Title.

HE2810.C2B47 1994   j385'09713'09034   C94-932089-7

Series design by Tania Craan
Cover and text design by Stephen Kenny
Cover illustration by Scott Cameron
Interior illustrations by Paul McCusker
Maps by James Loates
Editor: Peter Carver

Typesetting by M&S

The support of the Government of Ontario through the Ministry of Culture, Tourism and Recreation is acknowledged.

Printed and bound in Canada by Webcom Limited

McClelland & Stewart Inc.
The Canadian Publishers
481 University Avenue
Toronto, Ontario
M5G 2E9

1 2 3 4 5   98 97 96 95 94

CONTENTS

Maps appears on pages 8 and 66.

The events in this book actually happened as told here. Nothing has been made up. This is a work of non-fiction and there is archival evidence for every story and, indeed, every remark made in this book.

Adventures in Canadian History

STEEL ACROSS THE SHIELD

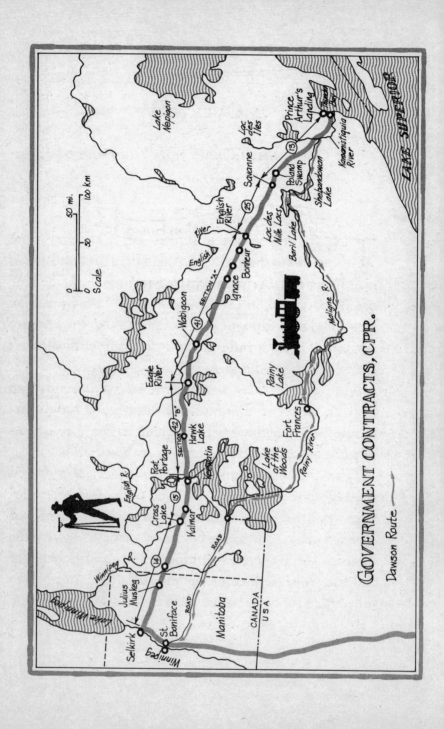

GOVERNMENT CONTRACTS, C.P.R.

Dawson Route ——→

LAKE SUPERIOR

Lake Nepigon

Lac des Iles

Prince Arthur's Landing

Thunder Bay

Savanne

Island Swamp

Kaministiquia River

Shebandowan Lake

English River

Lac des Mille Lacs

Bonil Lake

English River

Bonheur

Ignace

Mattague R.

Wabigoon

Eagle River

Rainy Lake

Fort Frances

Hawk Lake

Keewatin

Lake of the Woods

Rainy River

English R.

Rat Portage

Cross Lake

Valmar

Winnipeg

Julius Muskeg

St. Boniface

ROAD

ROAD

Manitoba

CANADA

USA

Selkirk

Winnipeg

Lake Winnipeg

SECTION "A"

SECTION "B"

Scale

0   50   100 km

50 mi.

50

OVERVIEW

One thousand miles of rock and muskeg

THE STORY OF THE BUILDING OF A RAILWAY from Ontario to the Pacific Ocean in the 1870s and 1880s is also the story of the creation of a new Canada. At the time of Confederation, in 1867, there was no "West" as we now know it. From a population point of view, the country stopped at Ottawa and did not begin again until the west coast of British Columbia.

Most people didn't believe that this vast, empty gap between the tiny communities of Victoria and New Westminster and the growing cities of the East could be crossed by a line of steel. There were too many barriers.

First, a thousand-mile (1,600 km) desert of rock and muskeg stood in the way – the roots of the ancient mountains we call the Canadian Shield. Next, a thousand miles of waving buffalo grass had to be crossed – empty country, the domain of only a handful of trappers and nomadic bands of Indians. Finally, three mountain walls, each nearly two miles (3.2 km) high, barred the way. Only after these were conquered could the wrinkled British Columbia coast be reached.

But if British Columbia was to be part of the new Dominion, and if the prairie country was to be filled with farmers, then somebody – government or private contractor – would have to build a railway to the Pacific. It would be a steel band joining up with the other railways in the East to bind the country together.

In the days before the automobile and airplane, the railway was king. But the project to build a Pacific line was fraught with danger. Hundreds of men would die blasting the railway through the mountains, bridging the muskegs and canyons, and hammering their way across the ancient rock of the Shield.

The Shield! It barred the way to the fertile plains – 700 miles (1,120 km) of the hardest and most ancient rock in the world, followed by 300 miles (480 km) of swamps so treacherous they could swallow locomotives at a single gulp.

This vast ocean of rocks, older than time, is the anchor that holds North America together. But it also splits Canada in two. No covered wagon could cross it; no immigrant could farm it, which explains why so many would-be Canadians moved into the United States to follow easier routes to the prairies.

Today when we drive the Trans-Canada Highway out of Toronto and North Bay, we are both awed and surprised by the raw beauty of this rocky desert, which our landscape painters have already made famous. In our comfortable automobiles we travel through a dark and haunting land of stunted pines and spruce, little gunmetal lakes, and Persian carpets of moss and lichen. Here we can sense the problems the early railway builders faced. And we can also see why another eighty years went by before this second link could be forged from sea to sea – today's Trans-Canada Highway.

Back in 1871, Prime Minister John A. Macdonald had promised British Columbia a railway. But Macdonald was driven from office two years later, and a more cautious Liberal prime minister, a solemn stonemason, Alexander Mackenzie, scrapped Macdonald's ambitious scheme. He wanted to do the job on the cheap, using the Great Lakes as a water highway to substitute for the line of steel. Beyond the lakes he planned to hire contractors to build a railway in sections from Lake Superior to the Red River. After that, he felt, a simple wagon road could do the job across the plains.

And so the story of the building of the railway across the Canadian Shield, from the end of steel at North Bay to Selkirk (near the future site of Winnipeg), is a stop-and-go tale. The line was built in bits and pieces, first by the Mackenzie government and later, when Macdonald returned to power, by a private company, the Canadian Pacific Railway (CPR).

This is the story of two separate railways built across the Shield. One led west out of North Bay heading for Lake

Superior. The other, to which the first segment would eventually be linked, started at Fort William and moved west in fits and starts toward Selkirk.

Those two lines, blasted from the ancient rock and floated over vast swamps, were designed to link up with each other and with the line being driven across the plains and over the mountains to the Pacific.

This is also the story of Canada's beginnings, from a small, constricted country centred around the St. Lawrence valley to a transcontinental nation stretching between two oceans. Without the railway, Canada, as we know it, would not exist.

CHAPTER ONE

～

Bogs without bottom

Accoording to harry armstrong, a resident engineer for the railroad in the mid-1870s, the "construction of Canada's greatest highway [began] at a dead end." He was right. One chunk of the railway began at Red River and ran east toward the muskegs on the Ontario/Manitoba border. Another was built westward from Fort William literally to nowhere. These two pieces were useless because they didn't connect.

A third chunk of railway from Lake Nipissing to Thunder Bay had not even been considered and would not be started until the government got out of the railway business in 1881, turning construction over to a private company, the Canadian Pacific Railway (CPR).

Our story, therefore, is about the building of three railways that would eventually become one. Each line stretched across isolated, unpopulated country – so empty of people that Harry Armstrong, who lived along the half-completed line out of Fort William, had to trudge fifteen miles (24 km) to work and back again each day. His nearest neighbour lived nine miles (14.4 km) away. Without any doctoring he had to act as a midwife at the birth of his first child. Like everybody else, he fought off the mosquitoes and blackflies rising from the stinking, half-frozen swamps in clouds so thick they blotted out the sun.

This was the empty heart of Canada. The country was scarcely explored. There was no rail transportation to supply the railway builders. The contractors were forced to rely on steamers, flat boats, canoes, and barges to haul in supplies and construction materials.

At the end of the 1870s, when other contractors began to fill in the 181-mile (289.6 km) gap between the two useless lines of steel, every pound (0.45 kg) of goods had to come in over the lakes by canoe and portage because the end of steel was a good hundred miles (160 km) from Lake Superior. Steam shovels, horses, even locomotives and flat cars were hauled by sleigh in wintertime over frozen lakes, ice-sheathed granites, and snow-shrouded muskeg.

It was these muskegs – frozen masses of swamp and silt – that drove some railway contractors into bankruptcy. First, there were the notorious sinkholes – little lakes over which a thick crust of vegetable matter had formed and into which the line might tumble at any time. One, just north of Fort William, swallowed an entire train with a thousand feet (300 m) of track.

Sometimes new sinkholes would appear, even when the land seemed to be as solid as Gibraltar. When the railway builders tried to fill up the sinkholes with gravel, the frozen muskeg beneath would melt, and the entire foundation would heave and totter.

One giant swamp that thwarted the railway builders was the incredible Julius Muskeg, a vast bed of peat, six miles (9.6 km) across and of unknown depth. Here the naked trunks of dead trees protruded, their roots weaving a kind of blanket over a hidden jelly of mud and slime. Across these barriers, the railway builders built log mattresses, which were floated on top of the heaving bog. These contraptions of long interlaced timbers sometimes ran for a hundred feet (30 m).

Many of the lakes were equally treacherous. Their bottoms appeared solid, but actually consisted of more muskeg – muskeg so thick it swallowed up tons of earth and gravel, month after month.

One contractor who was defeated by the muskegs was Joseph Whitehead, mayor of Clinton, Ontario, and a Liberal member of Parliament from 1867 to 1872. He was an enormous Yorkshire man with a great bald dome of a head, a vast beard, and a big, fleshy nose, who had been a railwayman since boyhood.

Whitehead had the subcontract to build a section of the railway near Rat Portage (present-day Kenora) but he saw his dreamed-of profits slowly pouring into Cross Lake, a notorious swamp. Alas, for him, it gobbled up 220,000 yards (198,000 m) of gravel at a cost of $80,000. And even then the line continued to sink into the morass.

It had seemed so easy to Whitehead! He thought he

could simply carry his line of steel across a narrow expanse of water. Yet, ton after ton of sand and gravel vanished into that monstrous gulf. Every time he tried to build an embankment five or six feet (1.5 or 1.8 m) above the water, the lake would take a gulp and the entire mass would vanish beneath the waves. It bankrupted him.

After Whitehead's downfall, his section was taken over by a colourful Galway Irishman named Michael J. Haney, a lean, hard man with high cheekbones and a drooping moustache. Armstrong described him as "a rushing, devil-may-care chap who did things just as he chose without regard to authority." But the job almost did Haney in.

He risked his life many times. At one point he drained an entire lake and laid a mattress of timber across the mud bottom to carry the track. The rails were laid; the track looked firm; then, slowly, it began to sink.

His engineer refused to take a locomotive across this heaving mass. Haney announced he would do it himself. As he did, the log mattress sank deeper. The engine tilted wildly. Haney tried to back up but now the rails were at such an angle he could scarcely coax it up the incline, which was growing steeper by the minute. By sanding the rails for a better grip he was able to save himself, but only at the last minute.

Like the other contractors along the unfinished line, Haney faced the problem of alcoholism among his workers – "navvies," as they were called. There was a good reason for this. When they were not laying track across the soft porridge of the muskegs, they were blasting it through some of the hardest rock in the world – rock that rolled endlessly on, ridge after spiky ridge, like waves in a sullen ocean. That rock had to be blasted with nitroglycerine, the most unstable of explosives. Because every man who worked with explosives was in danger of his life, he drank to bolster his spirits.

Nobody seemed to care about safety regulations. Cans of nitroglycerine with fuses attached were strewn carelessly along the roadbed. They were carried about with such recklessness that the fluid itself splashed upon the rocks. Whole gangs were sometimes blown to bits in the explosions that followed.

If a container of nitroglycerine was shaken badly, it would explode. It couldn't be transported by wagons because the jarring along those trails would have caused disaster. The explosive had to be carried in ten-gallon (45 L) tins on men's backs.

This caused problems. Sometimes the packers would lay their tins down on a smooth rock and a few drops would be left behind from a leak. The engineers travelling up and down the line tried to avoid these telltale black specks, which could easily blow a man's leg off. Once, when a teamster took his horse to water at such a spot, the horse's iron shoe touched a pool of nitroglycerine. The resulting blast tore the shoe from his foot and drove it through his belly, killing him and stunning the teamster.

Blasting the rock of the Canadian Shield was a dangerous task.

The number of men killed or maimed by such explosions was staggering. In one fifty-mile (80 km) stretch there were thirty graves, all the result of the careless handling of nitroglycerine. And yet the Irish navvies joked among themselves about the danger, often tripping gaily down a hill, each with a can of liquid explosive on his back, and making comments all the while:

"It's a warm day."

"That's so, but maybe ye'll be warmer before ye camp tonight."

"That's so. D'ye want any work taken to the Devil?"

"To hell, I guess."

"Take another train and keep a berth for me, man!"

"Is that ye're coffin, ye're carrying, Pat?"

"Faith, ye're right; and the coroner's inquest to the bargain, Jim."

A woman who watched this scene wrote that, in spite of the jokes, "the wretched expression of these very men proved that they felt the bitterness of death to be in their chests."

There were terrible accidents. One young man, climbing a hill with a can of explosives, stumbled and fell. All they found of him was his foot in a tree a hundred yards (90 m) away. Another man's foot slipped as he handed a can of nitroglycerine to a driller. As a result, four men died and three more were maimed. One workman brushed past a rock where some explosive had been spilled. He lost his arm and his sight in an instant. At Prince Arthur's Landing at

Lakehead, an entire nitroglycerine factory blew up in the night, hurling chunks of frozen earth for a quarter of a mile (0.4 km) , and leaving a hole twenty feet (6 m) deep and fifty feet (15 m) across.

No wonder the navvies along the line turned to alcohol! As Haney himself recalled, "There was not an engineer, contractor, or traveller who were not hard drinkers. Practically every transaction was consummated with a glass."

The contractors tried – without success – to keep the camps dry, but the whisky pedlars had kegs of liquor concealed at points along the entire right of way. The profits were huge. A gallon (4.5 L) of alcohol, worth 50¢ in the eastern cities, could sell for $45 on the line. Hidden out in the bush or on the islands that dotted the swampy lakes, the pedlars moved into the work camps in swift canoes of birchbark, then darted away at the approach of the law.

Haney made no attempt to stop this traffic – except when his men worked three round-the-clock shifts. At such times he would round up the whisky pedlars and get them to promise to stay away as long as the twenty-four-hour shift prevailed.

Generally this secret agreement worked. On one occasion, however, the presence of 500 thirsty men was too much for the whisky pedlars. Haney came to work to find the whole camp roaring drunk. He moved quickly. There were four "whisky detectives" working on his section. Haney warned them that unless the pedlars were brought before him by noon, all four would be fired. That did it. The offenders were rounded up, fined a total of $3,600, and packed back to Winnipeg, with a warning that if they came back, they'd be jailed.

CHAPTER TWO

~

Gunplay at Rat Portage

B Y THE TIME MICHAEL HANEY ARRIVED ON the scene at the end of the 1870s, the solemn, unknown land through which Harry Armstrong had trudged on his fifteen-mile (24 km) trek to the job site had come alive with thousands of navvies – Swedes, Norwegians, Finns and Icelanders, French Canadians and Prince Edward Islanders, Irish, Scots, English, Americans, and even Mennonites – all strung out over nearly five hundred miles (800 km) in clustered, hard-drinking communities.

The postmaster of Whitemouth, the railroad community halfway between Winnipeg and Rat Portage, described Christmas Eve in 1880: "The demon of strong drink made a bedlam of this place, fighting, stabbing, and breaking; some lay out freezing till life was almost extinct. The Post Office was besieged at the hours of crowded business by outrageous, bleeding, drunken, fighting men, mad with Forty-Rod, so that respectable people could not come in for their mail.... It is only a few days since in one of these frenzies a man had his jugular nearly severed by a man with a razor."

Because such communities only lasted a year or so, political organization was difficult. In July 1880, for instance, when the end of track moved beyond Gull River to Ignace, all the inhabitants had to move – stores, houses, boarding houses, a jewellery shop, a hotel, a telegraph office, a shoemaker, and a blacksmith shop.

The only permanent town along the half-built line, and by far the largest, was Rat Portage on Lake of the Woods. It called itself "the Future Saratoga of America" – a reference to that famous vacation spot in the eastern United States. It was nothing of the sort. We know it today as Kenora, and in its heyday it was the wildest community in Canada.

One newspaper correspondent summed it up in the summer of 1880 when he wrote: "For some time now the railway works in the vicinity of Rat Portage have been besieged by a lot of scoundrels whose only avocation seems to be gambling and trading in illicit whisky, and the state of degradation was, if anything, intensified by the appearance, in the wake of these blacklegs, of a number of the *demi-monde* with whom these numerous desperadoes held high carnival at all hours of the day or night."

One observer described the town as being "laid out in designs made by a colony of muskrats." Shanties and tents were built or pitched wherever the owners wanted and without any organization of streets or roadways. It had a floating population that sometimes reached as high as 3,000. The contractors of Section B on the railway ran the administration, built the jail, and organized the police. There was no real law.

In 1881, Manitoba's borders were extended and nobody was sure whether Rat Portage was in Manitoba or Ontario. Both provinces built jails and appointed magistrates and constables, and so did Ottawa. For a while it was more dangerous to be a policeman than a lawbreaker. Policemen began arresting each other until the jails were full of opposing lawmen.

Ontario constables were kidnapped and shipped to Winnipeg. The Manitoba jail was set on fire. Anybody who wished to could become a policeman. He was given free whisky and special pay, because the job was so dangerous.

For a time some of the toughest characters in Rat Portage – with names like Black Jim Reddy of Montana, Charlie Bull-Pup, Boston O'Brien the Slugger, Mulligan the Hardest Case – were actually acting as policemen.

In 1883, both provinces called elections on the same day, and both premiers campaigned in Rat Portage. That election was certainly rigged: the premier of Manitoba actually got more votes than there were voters! The confusion didn't end until 1884, when the town was officially declared to be part of Ontario.

Rat Portage was the headquarters for the illegal liquor industry, with 800 gallons (3,600 L) pouring into town every month. The booze was hidden in oatmeal and bean sacks or disguised as barrels of coal oil. For every thirty residents, one was a whisky pedlar. "Forty-Rod," so called because it was claimed it could drop a man at that distance, sold for the same price as champagne in Winnipeg. Illegal saloons operated on the islands that speckled the Lake of the Woods.

Attempts at prohibition brought in gun-toting mobsters, corrupt officials, and harassed police. One bloody incident, in the summer of 1880, involved two whisky traders named Dan Harrington and Jim Mitchell. It had all the elements of a western gun battle.

Harrington and Mitchell had worked for Joseph Whitehead but soon abandoned him for the more lucrative trade of liquor peddling. A warrant was issued for their arrest, but when the constable tried to serve it, the two beat him brutally. At Rat Portage the magistrate was in their pay. They simply gave themselves up to him, were fined a total of $50, and got away. They headed east with fifty gallons (225 L) of whisky for a turbulent little community named Hawk Lake, where the railroad navvies had just been paid.

The company's constable found Harrington and Mitchell in front of Millie Watson's tent at Hawk Lake. Mitchell fled into the woods, but Harrington announced he'd sell whisky in spite of the police. The constable took his gun from him and placed him under arrest.

Harrington asked for permission to go inside the tent and wash up. There a friend handed him a brace of loaded seven-shot revolvers. He cocked the weapons and emerged from the tent with both guns pointed at the constable. Alas for him, the policeman was a fast draw. Before Harrington could fire, he shot him through the heart.

Harrington dropped to the ground and tried to retrieve his guns. A second constable told Ross not to bother to fire again; the first bullet had taken effect.

"You're damned right it has taken effect," Harrington snarled, "but I'd sooner be shot than fined." Those were his last words.

Now Archbishop Taché of St. Boniface decided the workers needed a permanent chaplain. For that task he selected the best known of all the voyageur priests, Father Albert Lacombe, one of the nomadic Oblate Order, who had spent most of his adult life among the Cree and Blackfoot of the Far West.

In November 1880, Lacombe set out reluctantly for his new parish. A homely man, whose long, silver locks never seemed to be combed, Lacombe didn't want to be a railway chaplain. But he went where he was told. Shocked by the language of the railroad navvies, Lacombe delivered an attack on blasphemy from his boxcar chapel as his first sermon.

"My God," he wrote in his diary, "have pity on this little village where so many crimes are committed every day." He soon realized he couldn't stop the evil, and so settled at last for prayer "to arrest the divine anger."

He moved up and down the line, covering thirty different camps, eating beans off tin plates in the mess halls,

Father Lacombe travelled to each camp in an open handcar.

preaching sermons as he went, celebrating mass in the mornings, talking and smoking with the navvies in the evenings, and recording on every page of his little tattered notebook a list of the sins committed among his flock.

Ill with pleurisy, forced to travel the track in an open handcar in the bitterest weather, his ears ringing with obscene phrases he had never before heard, his eyes offended by spectacles he didn't believe possible, he could only cry out to his diary, "My God, I offer you my sufferings." He was as hard as frozen pemmican, toughened by years of prairie travel, but he almost met his match in the rock and muskeg country.

"Please, God, send me back to my missions," he wrote. But it was not until the final spike was driven that his prayers were answered. He made more friends than he knew, however. When it was learned that he was leaving at last, the workmen of Section B took up a large collection and presented him with a generous assortment of gifts: a horse, a buggy, a complete harness, a new saddle, a tent, and an entire camping outfit to make his days on the plains more comfortable. Perhaps, as he took his leave, he felt that his mission to the godless had not been entirely in vain.

I N 1881, JOHN A. MACDONALD'S GOVERNMENT got out of the railroad business, and the newly-formed Canadian Pacific Railway Company took it over.

In addition to completing the unfinished sections between Red River and Lakehead, the CPR also contracted to build the line from Lakehead to its eastern terminus at Lake Nipissing. There it would connect with an already constructed line leading to Ottawa and the East.

The price of building the line north of Lake Superior was appalling. One ninety-mile (144 km) section of rails ate up $10 million. One single mile (1.6 km) of track was laid through solid rock at a cost of $700,000. By the summer of 1884, close to fifteen thousand men and four thousand horses were at work between Lake Nipissing and Thunder Bay. Every month the company sent out a pay car with $1,100,000 in wages.

The amount of explosives needed to blast through the cliffs was staggering. Three dynamite factories, each capable of turning out a ton (900 kg) a day, were built in the

Caldwell-Jackfish area near the north shore of Lake Superior. The bill for dynamite, nitroglycerine, and black powder came to $7.5 million.

The new line would hug the armoured shores of Lake Superior. Construction there would be heavy, but it would be easy to supply by lake boats especially built for the purpose.

Supplies were shipped forward from Georgian Bay and distributed at points a hundred miles (160 km) apart along the north shore of Superior. Rough portage roads were blasted out between each delivery point to bring provisions to the track layers. Most of that transportation had to be done in the winter when the lakes were frozen and the snow packed hard as cement. It took 300 dog teams to keep the railroad supplied.

The work went on winter and summer. Track had to be laid in all seasons – in snow five feet (1.5 m) deep and in temperatures that dropped to -40°F (-40°C). The drifts were often so high that nobody could find the centre line of the railroad. The rails were laid directly on top of the snow. Sometimes it was found, after the snow had melted, that the line as surveyed was in the wrong place.

William Cornelius Van Horne, the general manager of the railway, imported a new track-laying machine to speed up the work. This was really a train loaded with rails, ties, and track fastenings. High, open-top chutes with rollers spaced along the bottom were hung on either side. The ties and rails were then rolled along by manpower to the front, where they were manhandled onto the grade.

It was too expensive to cut through the hills and fill up the hollows with teams hauling rock and gravel away. Instead, Van Horne decided to build timber trestles over the valleys, gullies, and cliffs, and fill them in later when the trains themselves could carry the fill.

As always, the blasting of the Shield was done at the expense of men's lives. Although dynamite had replaced the more dangerous nitroglycerine, it too could be dangerous when carelessly handled. One man, for instance, who tried to pack a dynamite cartridge tighter by tamping it down with an iron crowbar was blown to pieces. A hotel proprietor from Port Arthur, out fishing, reached into the water and picked up a live discarded dynamite cap among the rocks. It blew off his hand. Once a rock from a blast tore through the roof of a cabin and killed a sleeping man.

The scenery, in words of Superintendent John Egan, was "sublime in its very wildness … magnificently grand." He wrote that, "God's own handiwork stands out boldly every furlong you proceed. The ravines and streams are numerous and all is picturesqueness itself." For those who had time to look beyond the hardships, the dark rocks tinted with the bright accents of lily, rose, and buttercup or the sullen little lakes wearing their yellow garlands of spatter-dock held a particularly Canadian beauty. But to the men on the job – throats choked with the dust of shattered rocks, ears ringing with dynamite blasts, arms aching from swinging sledges or carrying rails, skin smarting and itching from a hundred insect bites, nostrils assailed by a dozen stenches from horse manure to human sweat – the scenery was only a nuisance to be moved when it got in the way.

The summers were bad enough, with clouds of flies and mosquitoes tormenting everybody, but the winters were especially hard. In the flat light of December, the whole world took on a grey colour, and the cold wind blowing off the great frozen inland sea sliced through the thickest garments.

One railroad navvy gave this description of Christmas Day, 1883, at the end of track out of Port Arthur: "Somehow Christmas Day fell flat. Here and there a group were playing cards for ten-cent points. Some few melancholy-looking Englishmen were writing letters. I was smoking and cursing my stars for not being at home in the family group. I wondered how many men were in the same mood. Instead of having a good time, that Christmas afternoon was gloomy. Some of us turned it into Sunday and began darning socks and mitts. By and by a fair-haired boy from the old sod approached with a sigh: 'Where were you, old fellow, this time last year?'

"'Never mind,' I answered, 'Where were you?'"

The boy replied that he was driving his girl behind a spanking team to see his family. Then he blurted out the rest of the story. "It was an old tale. Someone drew a herring across his track, a fit of jealousy, etc., etc., which ended in his leaving home, and now he was sitting in the gloom beside a rough coon like me dressed only as a bushman or a railroader can dress and pouring into my ears a long love story."

The navvies lived in gloomy and airless bunkhouses that were little better than log dungeons. These were low-walled buildings, about sixty feet (18 m) long and thirty feet (9 m) wide, built of spruce logs, chinked with moss, and plastered with clay or lime.

Between sixty or eighty men were crammed into these hastily built buildings. They slept in lice-filled blankets on beds of hay in double-decker bunks. The ventilation was slight. A faint light entered from two small windows at either end – hardly enough to write or read by. At night steam rose from the wet clothes that hung over the central stove. In the summer the men burned straw and rags to drive off the maddening hordes of mosquitoes and black flies, and this thickened the air. Baths were unknown. Men washed or laundered their clothes or not as they wished. There was little medical attention.

Van Horne believed in feeding his men well, but the menu was often monotonous and unhealthy because of the difficulties in transportation. The only real delicacy was fresh bread. Otherwise, the staples were salt pork, corned beef, molasses, beans, potatoes, oatmeal, and tea, with the occasional bit of frozen beef. The lack of fresh meat or vege-tables and fruit made most men feel sluggish and weary. The conditions were so bad in those years that it was hard to

The navvies lived in gloomy, airless bunkhouses.

get men to work in this situation, and the pay wasn't much of an incentive. Shovel men only got a $1.50 for a ten-hour day and some as little as a $1 a day. Anybody who tried to start a union was fired.

Things grew better in the winter of 1883-84. Wages rose to $1.75 for a shovel man and $2 a day for a rock man. But board was boosted to $4 a week, and so the net pay was about the same.

Men were paid only for the days on which they worked. If weather or sickness or delays kept them in the bunk-houses, they got nothing. Eight wet days a month could reduce a man's net pay, after board was deducted, to $4 a week. Besides that, he had to buy his clothing and gear at the company store at inflated prices and sometimes his meals and transportation enroute to the site.

He had no options because the company controlled his shelter and transport. If he complained, he could be fired. If he wanted to quit, he had to pay his board and room until the company could get him out to civilization – and then he had to pay his fare. Under such a system it was hard for anybody to save much money.

Yet these conditions were much better than those of the men who worked for themselves in small subcontracts, grading short strips of right of way with shovel and wheel-barrow or clearing the line of brush and stumps for fixed prices arrived at by hard bargaining.

This work might involve only two partners, or even a group of a dozen or more. There was one advantage – the men were their own bosses; they could work or not as they wanted. But this wasn't much of an advantage, because most of them worked longer hours and under worse conditions than their fellow wage-earners and made no more money. The men who profited were the larger contractors who got the job done at a low cost.

The workmen here existed almost like animals in a cave. Harry Armstrong came upon one camp of French Canadians that he thought was the worst he had ever seen. They lived and slept in a windowless log hovel, lit by a candle made from a tin cup filled with grease and a rag as a wick. In one corner stood a cookstove, its smoke pouring out of a hole in the roof; in another corner, in the dim light, Armstrong could just make out a straw mattress occupied by an injured man waiting for a doctor.

There was no flooring, only a sea of black mud kept thawed by the heat of the stove. A few scattered poles lay across the mud over which the workmen were obliged to pick their way. If a man slipped off, he sank to his ankles in slime.

Armstrong hoped for something to eat. But all he got was some refuse from the table that had been scraped off after each meal. It was the best the French Canadians had to offer.

The Italian immigrants were even worse off. One group lived during the winter in a kind of root cellar without windows. To enter they crawled through an opening in the bottom. There they lay most of the time, playing cards, but going out into the snow when the sun shone to do a little work, clearing the brush along the line. Once a week they bought a sack of flour and a little tea on credit. By spring they had managed to clear half an acre (0.2 ha). The proceeds had hardly paid for their winter's provision and by then most were suffering badly from scurvy.

These hovels were in sharp contrast to the quarters of the major contractors, who lived in relative luxury. One man had a home complete with Brussels carpet and grand piano. Another had his own cow to dispense milk punches to his guests. And the contractors and senior engineers had their wives and children with them, thus escaping the loneliness of the bunkhouse.

Again, the navvies turned to alcohol to lighten their nights. The government had put through a special act, banning the sale of liquor along the line as far as Manitoba. But once again government agents fought a running battle with whisky pedlars.

In one section between Whitemouth River and Lake Wabigoon, some twenty-five hundred people managed to drink 800 gallons (3,600 L) of illegal spirits every month – at a cost of $15 a gallon. (In Toronto at that time the same whisky sold for as little as 50¢.)

The whisky pedlars were clever in deceiving the police, even going so far as to get the railway foremen drunk. Often they seized control of the local police force and controlled the town through a vigilante committee. Violence was not unusual. On the Lake Superior line a company count revealed that there were 5,000 revolvers, 300 shotguns and rifles, and the same number of dirks and bowie knives in the possession of railway workers.

In Michipicoten (near the present town of Wawa), the vigilante gang that ran the town was actually headed by a former police chief, Charles Wallace. In October 1884, this gang attempted to shoot the local magistrate, who took refuge in a construction office, ducking bullets fired through the walls. A force of Toronto police was called to restore order. They holed up in a local boarding house and arrested seven men. But the boarding house became the target of hidden riflemen who pumped bullets into it, grazing the arm of the cook, and narrowly missing one of the boarders.

When the police poured out of the building with revolvers drawn, the unseen attackers fled. It was said that forty men, armed with repeating rifles, were on their way to rescue the prisoners, but the police maintained an all-night vigil, and there was no further trouble.

They destroyed 120 gallons (540 L) of rye whisky and seized a sailboat used in the trade. Then they laid plans to capture the four ringleaders of the terrorist gang, including Wallace.

With the help of spies, they descended upon a nearby Indian village where the culprits were supposed to be hiding. They flushed out the wanted men, but Wallace and his friends were too fast for them. A chase followed but the hoodlums easily got away, apparently with the help of both the Indians and the townspeople.

No sooner had the big-city policemen left than Wallace and his three henchmen emerged and instituted a new reign of terror. Wallace was armed like a bandit, with four heavy revolvers, a bowie knife in his belt, and a Winchester repeating rifle on his shoulder. The gang boarded a lake steamer, pumped bullets into the crowd on the dock, and then left for Sault Ste. Marie. They weren't captured until the following February, after a gun fight in the snow in which one of the policemen was severely wounded. Wallace got eighteen months in prison, and by the time he got out of jail, the railway was finished, and the days of the whisky pedlars were over forever.

CHAPTER FOUR

~

Treasure in the rocks

WHEN THE CPR WAS BORN IN 1881, the line between Fort William and Selkirk was still not finished. In fact the line was so badly put together, it had to be rebuilt and relocated. But, by 1882, the gaps in the line between Winnipeg and Thunder Bay were finally closed.

But there was still no line of track between Thunder Bay and Lake Nipissing. The contractors, supplied by boat, were strung out in sections of varying lengths, depending on the ground. Indeed, some contracts were so difficult that some only covered one mile (1.6 km) of line.

The Lake Superior line was divided into two sections. The difficult section led east from Fort William to meet the easier section that ran west from Lake Nipissing. At Lake Nipissing the new railway joined the Canada Central Line out of Ottawa.

In the summer of 1882, a young eighteen-year-old Scot, John McIntyre Ferguson, arrived at Lake Nipissing. He was smart enough to buy 288 acres (115.2 ha) of land at a $1 an acre and to lay out a townsite in the forest. He built the first house in the region, and in ordering nails, asked the supplier to ship them to the "north bay of Lake Nipissing." Thus the settlement got its name. By 1884, North Bay was a thriving community. As for Ferguson, he went on to become the wealthiest man in town and later its mayor for four terms.

North Bay was the creation of the railway. Before its first buildings were put up, the main institutions were located in railway cars shunted onto sidings. The early church services were held in these cars. The preacher, a giant of a man named Silas Huntington, used an empty upended barrel as a pulpit and brooked no opposition from the rougher elements in his congregation. When two muscular navvies disagreed with one of his sermons, Huntington left his barrel pulpit and started toward them, preaching as he went. As he drew opposite the intruders, he took one in each hand and dropped them out of the door, without pausing for breath, or halting the flow of his sermon.

On another occasion when Huntington's boxcar church was parked at a siding on a hillside, somebody accidentally released the brake. As Huntington was in the middle of his sermon, the car gave a jerk and slowly rolled downhill, gathering speed as it went. It ran down to the main line and off to the edge of the new town. But Huntington, without raising an eyebrow, continued his sermon. When he finished, the congregation sang "O God From Whom All Blessings Flow" and walked back without comment.

All the land between North Bay and Lake Superior was

NAVVIES BLOW OFF STEAM AT TENT COMMUNITIES ALONG THE LINE

CONVEYOR BELT

ROLLERS

THE TRACK LAYING MACHINE

THE RAILS WERE DROPPED ONTO THE CONVEYOR BELT AND SLID ALONG WHERE THEY WERE PUT INTO POSITION ON THE TIES.

thought to be worthless wilderness. Many politicians had opposed the idea of building a railway over the bleak rocks and through the stunted forests of the Shield country. Why would any sane man want to run a line of steel through such a dreadful country? But John A. Macdonald insisted on an all-Canadian line.

The rails, moving westward from North Bay, cut through a barren realm, blackened by forest fires and empty of colour, save for the occasional dark reds and yellows which stained the rocks and glinted up through the roots of the dried grasses on the hillsides. These were actually the oxides of nickel and copper and the sulphides of copper and iron. But it needed a trained eye to detect the signs of treasure that lay concealed beneath the charred forest floor.

By the end of 1882, the Canada Central Railway reached Lake Nipissing. By the end of the following year, the first 100 miles (160 km) of the connecting CPR were completed. Early that year the crudest of roads, all stumps and mud, had reached the spot where Sudbury stands today. And there, as much as by accident as by design, a temporary construction camp was established.

This was entirely a company town. Every boarding house, home, and store was built, owned, and operated by the CPR to keep the whisky pedlars at bay. Even the post office was on company land. And the company store-keeper, who later became Sudbury's first mayor, acted as postmaster.

On the outskirts of town, private merchants hovered

about hawking their goods from packs on their backs. It wasn't until 1884 that the most enterprising of these, a firm-jawed pedlar named John Frawley, discovered that the CPR did not own all the land after all. The Jesuit priests had been on the spot for more than a decade and held title to it. Frawley leased a plot of land from the religious order for $3 a month, opened a men's furnishing store in a tent, and broke the company monopoly. By then a mining rush was in full swing, and Sudbury was on its way to becoming a permanent community.

A CPR blacksmith, Tom Flanagan, was the first to suspect there might be treasure hidden in the rocks. He picked up a piece of yellow bronze ore about three miles (4.8 km) from town and thought he had found gold. He was wrong. He had no idea he was standing not only on a rich copper mine but also on the largest nickel deposit in the world.

It would be nice to report that Flanagan became a millionaire as a result. Unfortunately, he did nothing about his find. But John Loughlin, a contractor cutting railway ties, was interested by the formations. He brought in three friends, Tom and William Murray, and Harry Abbott. In February 1884, they staked the land on what became the future Murray Mine of the International Nickel Company. It was to produce ore worth millions – but not for the original discoverers.

Some company employees became rich, however. One was a gaunt Hertfordshire man named Charles Francis Crean. He had been working on boats along the upper

Ottawa carrying supplies to construction camps. He arrived on the first work train into Sudbury on November 23 at a time when the settlement hadn't even been surveyed. The buildings were being thrown together and laid out with no thought for the future. The first log hospital turned out to be in the middle of what later became the junction of Logan and Elm Streets. The mud was so bad that a boy actually drowned in a hole in the road opposite the American Hotel.

On his arrival, Crean walked into the company store and saw a huge yellow nugget being used as a paper weight. The clerk thought the ore probably contained iron pyrites – fool's gold – but he gave Crean a piece of it. Crean sent it to a chemist friend in Toronto who told him it was an excellent sample of copper. In May 1884, Crean applied for a mining claim and staked what was to become famous as the Elsie Mine.

A month later, the observant Crean spotted some copper ore in the ballast along the tracks of the Sault Ste. Marie branch of the railroad. He checked back carefully to find where it came from and was able to stake that property. On this spot, another rich mine, the Worthington, was established. Later Crean discovered three other valuable properties, all of them steady producers.

A week after Crean staked his first claim, a timber prospector, Rinaldo McConnell, staked some further property which was to become the nucleus of the Canadian Copper Company's Sudbury operation – the forerunner of the

International Nickel Company. It was copper, of course, that attracted the miners; nickel had few uses in those days.

Another prospective millionaire was a timekeeper named Thomas Frood, a onetime druggist and school teacher from southwestern Ontario. He acted on a trapper's hunch and discovered the property that became the most famous of all – the Frood Mine.

The story of northern Ontario mining – and, in particular, Sudbury – is a story of accident, coincidence, and sheer blind luck. The railway line was supposed to be located south of Lost Lake. The locating engineer decided to run it north. Sudbury wasn't even seen as a permanent community – just an unimportant spot on the map.

Thus, the politicians who had scoffed at the idea of a line running across the Shield were proved wrong. Alexander Mackenzie, when he was leader of the Opposition, had said it was "one of the most foolish things that could be imagined." His colleague, Edward Blake, seconded that comment. Indeed, right to the moment of Sudbury's founding, some members of John A. Macdonald's cabinet, as well as a couple of the CPR's own directors, were opposed to the line across the Shield. It was only when the land began to yield up its treasure that the fuss about an all-Canadian line came to an end.

CHAPTER FIVE

~

Rebellion!

B Y 1885, THE CANADIAN PACIFIC RAILWAY Company was on the edge of financial collapse. North of Lake Superior, Van Horne was desperately trying to link up the gaps between the isolated stretches of steel. These gaps totalled 254 miles (406.4 km). Until they were completed, the CPR could not begin its operation as a through road and start making money.

The government, pressed by its opponents, did not think it politically possible to guarantee any more loans to the CPR. Some kind of miracle would be needed to show how valuable a transcontinental railway would be to Canada. And in 1885, just as the company was foundering, the miracle occurred in the shape of Louis Riel.

In the North West, the railway had become a symbol of the passing of the Good Old Days. To the Indians, it was a new kind of boundary, solid as a wall. To the white settlers of northern Saskatchewan, it meant disappointment, because the CPR had refused to build the railway through the settled areas, preferring to drive the steel farther south where no settlements existed. To the farmers, the CPR spelled monopoly and grinding freight rates. To the mixed bloods of the Red River and northern Saskatchewan, it stood for revolutionary social change.

The people of the North West were stirred up from Winnipeg to Edmonton. Whites, Indians, and mixed bloods were all organizing. At the end of July 1884, the Crees of North Saskatchewan were welded into an Indian council by Big Bear, the most independent of the chiefs.

The Indians believed that the government had betrayed and deceived them, and they were right. Ottawa had promised to save them from starvation, but only one treaty spelled that out. Already their slim rations had been cut back as part of an official policy of saving money. It was plain that the politicians of the East had little understanding of conditions in the North West. Western newspapers supported the Indians, reporting that they were dying by the scores as the result of semi-starvation, resulting from the bad quality of food supplied by the government agencies.

The white settlers were angry too. The Manitoba Farmers' Union was threatening to pull out of Confederation, even to rebel. Other organizations were demanding that Ottawa change its attitude to the West. All these people wanted to run their own affairs, to reform the land laws, to control their own railways, to reduce the taxes on farm equipment imported from the United States, and to end the CPR monopoly.

The mixed bloods – the English, Scots, and the French-speaking Roman Catholic Métis – had another grievance. In the North West Territories they wanted what the government had recognized and granted in Manitoba in 1870 – a share in the aboriginal title to the land. They had been vainly petitioning Ottawa for this since 1873 but had been put off time after time.

A distinct community of Métis had been forming on the prairies as the mixed bloods struggled to maintain their identity. As the Moose Jaw *News* reported in April 1884, the Métis "have been driven by the inevitable back and aback, like their half-brothers, the red men of the continent.... What is their future?"

By the spring of 1884, protest meetings were becoming common at St. Laurent, the strongest and best established of the Métis communities, near Duck Lake on the South Saskatchewan River. In May 1884, one Métis wrote to Louis Riel (who had been exiled after the North West uprising in 1871) that the North West Territories "were like a volcanoe ready to erupt. The excitement is almost general. All minds are everywhere excited. Since the month of March last public meetings are everywhere frequently held ... French and English Half-breeds are now united.... On all sides people complain of injustice; they invoke equity, they desire to obtain our rights."

By then the united community on the forks of the Saskatchewan had decided Riel was the only man who could lead them – peacefully, it was hoped – in a campaign to force the government's hand. Fifteen years before, he had been a champion for his people in an uprising that turned him into a martyr and laid the groundwork for the formation of a new province – Manitoba. Now the Métis leaders were determined to talk Riel into repeating that triumph. No one else had his magnetic personality, his sense of tactics, his eloquence and, above all, his reputation.

In the spring of 1884, Gabriel Dumont, the most popular and respected man along the Saskatchewan, set off to see Riel with three other Métis delegates. Dumont, at forty-seven, was a swarthy, stocky man with bold shoulders and a handsome, kindly face. He had been chief of his people since the age of twenty-five, much beloved by all who knew him, including the Mounted Police.

Dumont and his followers arrived at Riel's small home in Montana on June 4, 1884. Riel was living in poverty. Canada, he believed, owed him both land and money as the result of the settlement made when Manitoba was created in 1871. He promised the delegation he would return to Canada to fight not only for his personal rights and those of his people but also for the white settlers and the Indians.

It was this decision that led to the bloody events of March 1885 that touched off the Saskatchewan Rebellion. The blood was spilled at Duck Lake on March 25 when, during a parley with Dumont and his men, the impatience of the police provoked a skirmish. The Métis won. Half an hour later, ten members of the mixed government force of police and volunteers lay dead. Thirteen more were wounded, two mortally. The Métis suffered only five casualties. The Saskatchewan Rebellion had begun.

Meanwhile, in Ottawa, John A. Macdonald had for some time been concerned about the situation in the North West – but not concerned enough to do anything about the Métis demands. He knew that some sort of outbreak was possible and could only wish that the CPR was completed. It wasn't. By the beginning of March, the number of gaps in the line had been reduced to four, but these still totalled eighty-six miles (137.6 km). Between these unconnected strips of track – much of it unballasted and laid hastily on top of the snow – was a frozen waste of forest, rock, hummocky drifts, whipped up by the icy winds that shrieked in from the lake.

Macdonald was preparing a force to go out west to keep order, but how would they get there? William Van Horne knew how. He asked the prime minister to tell him when the government might expect to have the troops ready. Macdonald figured that it might be in the first or second week in March. Van Horne made an instant decision. He pledged he could get troops from Kingston or Quebec all the way to Saskatchewan in just ten days.

Van Horne could see how valuable the railway would be if a rebellion broke out in the prairies. The hard-pressed CPR could only benefit. How could the government refuse to aid a railway if it sped troops out west, took the Métis unaware, and crushed a rebellion? He immediately offered the Privy Council the services of his railway to move the troops. There was just one condition: he and not the army was to be in complete control of food and transport.

It sounded like a foolhardy promise. Could men, horses, artillery pieces, and military supplies be shuttled over the primitive roads that crossed this blizzard-swept land? The members of Macdonald's council refused to believe it.

"Has anyone got a better plan?" Macdonald asked. There was no answer. And so Van Horne was told to get ready to move a massive amount of men, animals, arms, and equipment over the Shield.

On March 23, the first suggestion of a coming rebellion appeared in the Ontario newspapers. The next day Van Horne had his plan in operation. He told his deputy, Harry Abbott, to get ready to move 400 men as far as the end of track at Dog Lake, west of Sudbury.

Joseph Caron, the minister of militia and defence, wasn't sure the plan would work. "How can men and horse cross Nepigon – answer immediately," he wired Van Horne. Van Horne replied that it could be done.

On March 25, Abbott reported that he was ready. John Ross, in charge of the western section of the unfinished line, was also ready and didn't expect there would be any delays. That same day the clash at Duck Lake took place. When that news burst upon the capital, the country was immediately mobilized. And Caron told Abbott that the first troops would be ready to move on March 28.

In Ottawa, George Stephen, the president of the company, wanted to quit. The CPR was out of money, and there was nothing more he could do. Only if Van Horne's gamble worked would the politicians and the public realize how valuable an asset a transcontinental line could be. It could bind the nation together in time of trouble. Perhaps then the government would be prepared to guarantee a loan to the faltering railway.

Southern Canada learned from its newspapers on March 27 that a bloody rebellion had broken out in the North West. Once the Indians learned of the Métis' victory at Duck Lake, they joined the rebellion. Prince Albert, Fort Carlton, Batoche, Fort Pitt, even perhaps Fort Qu'Appelle, Calgary, Edmonton, Moose Jaw, and Regina were all threatened.

A wave of anger, patriotism, and excitement washed over eastern Canada. The government had called out the only permanent force in all of Canada – two artillery batteries stationed at Quebec and Kingston. That same day several militia regiments were ordered to be ready to move immediately to the North West.

But how on earth would they get there, people asked. In Kingston, the *British Whig* pointed out that if the soldiers travelled through the United States they would have to be disarmed. They would have to wear civilian clothes as private citizens, with their rifles and artillery pieces boxed for separate shipment to Winnipeg.

There was a rumour, however, that this passage might be avoided by going over the partially completed Canadian Pacific Railway. That possibility was considered very remote. How could troops, baggage, guns, horses, and equipment be shuttled over those trackless gaps?

The newspaper pointed out that a man who had recently travelled through the country and was asked how long it would take to cover the unrailed section laughingly replied, "Oh, until July." Another railwayman reported that there was at least four feet (1.2 m) of snow along the track and that "there would be considerable trouble getting through."

Van Horne was determined to move 3,324 men from London, Toronto, Kingston, Ottawa, Montreal, Quebec, Halifax, and a dozen smaller centres to the North West. Indeed, he expected to have the first troops in Winnipeg no more than ten days after the news of the Duck Lake engagement.

Neither Harry Abbott nor John Ross were worried. After all, they had been moving hundreds of workmen over the gaps in the line all that winter. When Abbott learned that the first 800 troops would arrive March 28, he was ready to receive them.

CHAPTER SIX

Marching as to war

NOW THE NEWS WAS OUT. The entire force was to be shipped west on the new railroad. A kind of frenzy seized the country. After all, the social life of the cities and towns revolved around the militia. Young officers were in demand at the winter sports that marked the era – the bobsled parties and skating fêtes and ice boat excursions and toboggan club outings.

The great social event of the year was the militia ball. And there were uniforms everywhere – at the opera house, at garrison theatricals, at afternoon teas. The tailors gave more attention to military fashions than to the civilian. The most popular weekend entertainment was watching the local militia parade through the streets or listening to a military band concert in the park.

Now, suddenly, these Saturday night soldiers were parading through the streets for the first time in earnest, for a country that had not yet fought a war of any kind. Never before had Canadians seen the kind of spectacular scenes that took place in every major town in the east during

March and April – the cheers for Queen and country, the blare of martial music, the oceans of flapping banners, the young men in scarlet and green marching behind the colours, the main streets jammed with waving thousands, the roll of drums, the troop trains puffing through the small towns – the singing, the cheering, the weeping and the kissing and the bitter goodbyes.

All this sound and spectacle, not to mention the military oratory that went with it, kept the country on an emotional binge for the better part of two weeks. This was true especially after April 2 when the news of the deaths of priests and civilians at Frog Lake at the hands of Big Bear's Indians filtered in to the cities.

The first units called out were the Queen's Own Rifles, the Royal Grenadiers, and the Infantry School of Toronto. The troops were required to be on parade by the morning of March 28. All that night, while the temperature hung around the freezing point, officers in hired carriages were rattling up and down the dark streets rousing their men. Long before dawn, the city was awake, thanks in part to the newly invented telephone, of which there were more than four hundred in the city.

Well before eight thirty on Saturday, West Market Street was jammed with people while the entrance to the drill shed on Jarvis Street was "filled up to the throat." Everybody was on hand to see the unaccustomed sight of militia men being called out and paraded for active service. Many had learned of their muster only on their way to work and came to the station in civilian clothes. Most believed they would be shipped directly to the North West. But now they were told they would not be leaving until Monday, March 30.

In the early hours of Monday morning, men in uniform began to pour into Toronto from the outlying centres. The main streets were crowded with would-be soldiers, many of whom arrived by streetcars, one claiming that he wanted to give that luxury a fond goodbye before heading west.

At the drill shed, the crowd was so dense that the soldiers themselves had trouble making their way through. The supply system was in disarray. The men had to supply their own boots, socks, shirts, and underwear – even their own lunch. Few had any idea of what was needed. Some came with extra boots in their hands. All had packs bulging with pies, rolls, and cooked meat. Some had tin cups hanging at their belts. Most were armed with a revolver of some kind stuck into a pocket. One enterprising salesman squeezed his way into the shed and began selling boots to those who had not thought to bring a second pair.

At eleven, Colonel William Dillon Otter spoke to the men, urging them to stay away from all drink and to throw away any bottles that they might have hidden in their kits. The troops cheered and pounded their rifle butts on the wooden floor.

Outside, the scenes were chaotic. The *Globe* reported that never in the history of Toronto had there been such a jam of people on King Street. It looked as if every citizen that could walk or crawl had come from miles around to line the route of the march. The street was a living, moving mass of humanity. The rooftops and cornices were alive with people who had waited hours to see the troops. Hundreds paid for positions in the flag-decked windows overlooking King Street. Women and children fainted continually and had to be removed by the police. Their nerves had become unstrung at the thought of their husbands, fathers, brothers, and sons leaving for the frontier. Many were weeping.

Then, at eleven thirty, there came a cheer from the troops in the shed. The mob outside – more than ten thousand people – broke into an answering cry. The cheer moved like a wave along King Street, so loud that the band of the 10th Royal Grenadiers could not be heard from half a block away. The crush made it impossible to move.

Somebody spotted the first uniform – that of a member of the Governor-General's Body Guard on horseback, followed by Colonel Otter, marching on foot at the head of his men. A group of about five hundred civilians rushed ahead clearing the way through the mass of spectators. And then could be seen the glittering brass of the band's instruments, the straight rows of fur caps, and the sharp outlines of rifles drifting above the craning heads.

Down the streets the young men came, as the crowd around them shouted themselves hoarse. Bouquets of flowers drifted from the windows above. Handkerchiefs fluttered. A thousand flags flapped in the breeze. Those who

The Canadian militia leaves Toronto for the West.

couldn't move along with troops began to cry "Goodbye, goodbye!" as the musicians struck up "The Girl I Left Behind Me." That was the theme song of Canada that month.

The crowd had been pouring in an unending stream to the foot of York Street by the station – all kinds and conditions of people in carriages and hacks, express vans, on foot, or pushing baby carriages – and all hoping to catch one last glimpse of brother, son, father, or sweetheart. The crowd jammed the Esplanade from one end of the station to the other, swarming over the roofs of freight cars and perching in every window. It began to rain, the rain becoming a heavy sleet, but the people didn't move.

Crammed into the cars, the men leaned out of windows and waved at the throng pressed up against the train. The cars began to crawl forward. Arms appeared waving final greetings. These were answered from the windows by an assortment of fluttering handkerchiefs, toques, forage caps, sidearms, socks, and even underwear. Then the band of the Queen's Own struck up "Auld Lang Syne," and as the engine bell began to ring, the men joined in.

These scenes were repeated over and over again in the following days. Everywhere the crowds were afire with excitement. In Montreal, when the French-speaking 65th Battalion paraded to the station, the crush was so great that a vast double window burst out from a three-storey building, injuring twelve people. In Quebec, the 9th Voltigeurs attended mass in the basilica and then marched through a wild crowd escorted by the city's snowshoe clubs in uniform, carrying torches. Never before had any of these cities seen such intense excitement.

Only the Governor-General's Body Guard, the oldest cavalry regiment in Canada, left in quiet and secrecy because the authorities feared for the safety of the seventy horses among the press of the crowds. They were kept ready to move for several days with very little sleep. And when they finally left shortly after midnight on April 7, their colonel, George T. Denison, and his officers had not slept for three nights, but remained booted and spurred for all that time, ready to move on the instant.

The press was enthusiastic about the condition of the troops. The Ottawa *Citizen,* describing one company of the Governor-General's Foot Guards, wrote that "it is one of the finest bodies of men for rough and ready service ever brought together in the Dominion."

That was substantially true. The men from the farms and the cities were hard muscled, keen, and young enough to laugh at the kind of ordeal they would shortly face along the uncompleted route to the CPR. But they were also woefully under-trained and under-equipped. The York Rangers, huddled in the Toronto drill shed, looked more like sheep than soldiers. In Kingston, it was noticed that members of the Composite Midland Regiment were badly drilled. There were men in the 65th in Montreal who had never fired so much as a blank cartridge.

Few battalions left for the North West properly

equipped. The belts and knapsacks of the Queen's Own had served in the Crimean War almost thirty years before. Their rifles were so old that they were mostly unreliable because of years of wear and tear. The clothing of the York Rangers was tattered and rotten, the knapsacks ill-fitting. Several of the Midland companies had no knapsacks at all and had to wrap their belongings in heavy paper. Others had no helmets. One outfit had no uniforms. Many of the 65th lacked trousers, tunics, and rifles. Even the crack Governor-General's Body Guard had not been issued satchels for their mounts; the men had been forced to wrap their personal belongings in blankets.

Until this moment, membership in the militia unit had been a social asset. Nobody had apparently ever considered the possibility that one day his unit would march off to war. The soldiers now had to depend on the generosity of the civilians. All the government was required to issue was a greatcoat, a tunic, trousers, and a rifle. Everything else was a soldier's own responsibility, and there was no provision made for wives and children left behind, although the civilians took up funds for the dependants.

The London town council supplied the volunteers with socks and underwear. A Montreal clothing firm gave the men of the 65th twenty-five dozen pairs of warm mittens. And, of course, there were bundles of bibles and second-hand books. At Almonte, a local storekeeper boarded a train with a more welcome gift – fifty packs of playing cards.

The trains sped off, two at a time, at staggered intervals, puffing through Carleton Place, Pembroke, North Bay, and Sudbury toward Dog Lake, where the real ordeal would begin. Van Horne insisted the officers be given first-class accommodation. He was determined that the image of the railway would be a good one. It was "important that the report of the officers as to the treatment of troops on our line should be favourable."

That's why the CPR was prepared to carry free any clothes or goods sent out to soldiers by friends or relatives. And Van Horne also made sure there would be mountains of food and gallons of hot, strong coffee along the way. He knew better than anybody what the troops were about to face. He couldn't protect them from the chill rides in open flat cars and sleighs, or for numbing treks across the glare ice, but he could make sure his army marched on a full stomach.

CHAPTER SEVEN

~

The cruel journey

As the cheering faded, the men from the cities, farms, and fishing villages of the East began to glimpse the rough face of the new Canada and to understand for the first time the real size of the country.

From North Bay the land stretched off to the horizon, barren and desolate, the spindly spruce rising in a ragged patchwork from the lifeless rock. The railway was completed for passenger traffic only as far as Biscotasing. Here the troops encountered the first of the CPR construction towns, a hard-drinking, backwoods village of log cabins. Just the day before the Queen's Own arrived, the police destroyed 500 gallons (2,250 L) of illicit whisky.

The first gap in the line began near Dog Lake, another construction camp not far from the site of present-day White River. Here the railway had prepared a marvellous dinner of beef, salmon, lobster, mackerel, potatoes, tomatoes, peas, beans, corn, peaches, currants, raisins, cranberries, fresh bread, cakes, pies, and all the tea and coffee they could drink. It was the last night of comfort that the

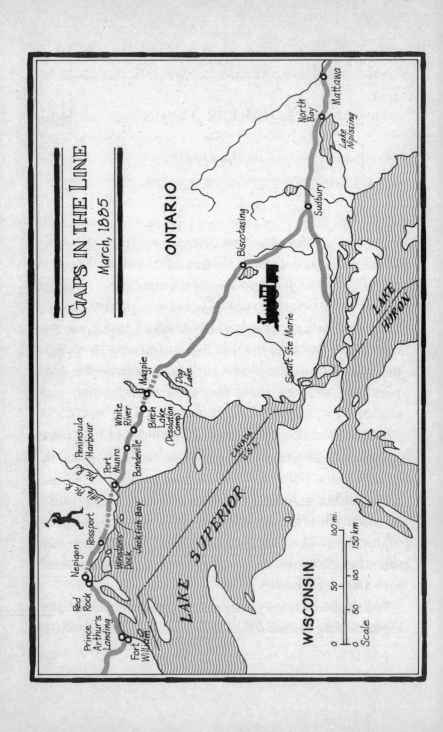

soldiers would know for several days. An adventure they would remember for the rest of their lives was about to begin.

They were packed tightly in groups of eight in sleighs and set off behind teams of horses down the uncompleted right of way. At every unbridged ravine and unfilled cut, the sleighs had to leave the graded surface, sometimes for miles, and follow the "tote road." This roller-coaster path cut through the forests, ran over stumps, windfalls, and rocks, dipped up and down gorges, and wound through seemingly impassable stretches of tightly packed trees.

At some points the sleighs encountered seven-foot boulders. At others they pitched into holes as deep as graves. The occupants were flung over the dashboards and into the haunches of the horses. Spills and accidents were so frequent they were taken as normal. One sleigh overturned no fewer than thirteen times in the forty miles (64 km) between Dog Lake and the end of track at Birch Lake.

Men who had been frozen in the -20°F (-29°C) weather were hurled out and swallowed up in six feet (1.8 m) of powdery snow, often with all of their equipment. Caps, mitts, mufflers, sidearms, and other articles of luggage were lost in the white blanket through which the sleighs reared and tumbled. One man was completely buried under an avalanche of baggage. A friend of his was nearly smothered when a horse fell on top of him.

The sleighs carrying the troops westward ran into empty sleighs turning eastward for a second load. Chaos resulted.

The detours were only wide enough to allow a single team to pass through without grazing the trees. If a horse got a foot or two (0.3 or 0.6 m) out of the track, the sleigh runners would lock onto a tree trunk, or, worse still, rise up on a stump, tilting occupants and baggage into the snow.

The trip was generally made by night, when the weather was cold enough to prevent the snow from turning into slush. The young soldiers crouched in the bottoms of the sleighs, wrapped in their greatcoats and covered with robes and blankets. But nothing could keep out the cold. To prevent themselves from freezing, officers and men would leap from the careering sleighs and trot alongside, trying to restore circulation. For some units, the cold was so intense that any man who left any part exposed, even for a few minutes, suffered frostbite.

At Magpie Point Camp – a halfway point along the unfinished right of way – the teams were changed. Here was more food. Many who arrived at Magpie thought that they had reached the end of their ordeal and were distressed when the bugle blew and they realized that it was only half over.

Scenes of confusion took place in the darkness. Men scrambled about seeking the sleighs to which they had been assigned. But the snow was dropping so thickly that friends could not recognize each other in the dark, with the horses whinnying and rearing, the Métis teamsters swearing, and the officers barking orders. The troops now realized that everything they owned was soaking wet and that they would have to endure four more hours of that bone-chilling journey.

Out of the yard the horses galloped along a route utterly unknown to them. They depended solely on their guides and their own instincts. Sometimes they tumbled, sleighs and all, over the high embankment, then righted themselves and plunged on. It took some nine hours to negotiate the gap between Dog Lake and Birch Lake. And at the end stood a lonely huddle of shacks which was swiftly named "Desolation Camp."

It certainly deserved its title. A fire had swept through the scrub timber, leaving the trees bleached a ghostly white. A cutting wind, rattling through these skeletal branches, added to the general feeling of despair. The only real shelter was a small tattered tent, not nearly large enough for those who tried to crowd in. Some men had to remain there for hours, their drenched clothing freezing to their skins in temperatures that dropped as low as -35°F (-37°C).

The 10th Royal Grenadiers arrived at Desolation Camp at five one morning after a sleigh journey that had begun at eight the previous evening. Because the trains weren't there to take them on, they had to endure a wait of seventeen hours. There wasn't even a fire to greet them. Tumbling out of the sleighs like ghosts – for the falling snow had covered them completely – they tried to huddle in the tent. It was so crowded that nobody could lie down.

Some men tried to light fires outside in three feet (0.9 m) of snow, only to see the embers disappear into deep holes melted through the crust. Others rolled themselves in their blankets like mummies and tried to sleep, the falling snow forming over them.

Every regiment that passed through Desolation Camp had its own story of hardship. Some members of the Queen's Own arrived hysterical from the cold and had to be led on board the cars, uncomprehending and uncaring. Although the troops had very little sleep when they arrived, they couldn't sleep at Desolation Camp because that meant certain death from freezing. The last battalion to arrive from Halifax had to endure a freezing rain, which soaked their garments and turned their greatcoats into boards. When a man dropped in his tracks, a guard was ordered to rouse him by any means, pulling him to his feet, kicking him, and bringing him over to the fires to dry. There the men stood, shivering and half-conscious, until the flat cars arrived.

In these roofless cars – the same open gravel cars used by construction crews to fill the cuts – sleep was impossible. Rough boards had been placed along the sides to a height of about six feet (1.8 m) and were held in place by stakes and sockets. Wind and snow blew into the crevices between the planks. Rough benches ran lengthwise and here the men sat, each with his blankets, packed tightly together, or huddled lengthwise on the floor.

For the Governor-General's Body Guard, such a journey was complicated by the presence of horses. There were no platforms or gangways to take the animals off the train. The men were obliged to gather railway ties and build little inclined planes up which the horses could be led. The snow was generally three or four feet (0.9 or 1.2 m) deep. The ties were sheathed in ice. The makeshift ramps had to be covered with blankets so the animals wouldn't lose their footing. And all had to be watered and fed before the men themselves could rest.

Because the horses couldn't be moved by sleigh across the Dog Lake gap to Desolation Camp, the cavalry men rode or led their horses the entire distance. When the cavalry moved by train, the horses were placed in the exactly the same kind of flat cars as the men. It took hours to unload them, because all their hind shoes had to be removed to prevent injuries to men and steeds.

The artillery had its own problems. It wasn't easy to load the nine-pound (4 kg) guns onto the flat cars. At one construction camp, four husky track layers were assigned to the job. One ran a crowbar into the muzzle of a cannon to get purchase, an act that caused the major in charge to fly into a rage. He fired the men, called for twenty of his own soldiers to tie a rope around the breech and, with great difficulty, managed to get it hauled up an inclined platform and onto the car.

It was a relief, after that, to leave Desolation Camp behind, but the ordeal was by no means over. Three more gaps in the line lay ahead and the worst was yet to come.

CHAPTER EIGHT

End of the line

FROM DESOLATION CAMP THE TRACK led on to the next gap at Port Munro. Here the ties had been laid directly onto the snow. In some sections where a thaw set in, four or five ties in succession, spiked to the rails, would be held off the ground for several inches.

One man said that the train's movement over those ties was like that of a birchbark canoe. Trains were thrown off this section of the track daily, and the rails were slowly being bent by the heavy passage. The trains rarely exceeded five miles (8 km) an hour, and so the men faced the longest night yet.

The Grenadiers, packed so closely together, took advantage of the mutual body warmth. Unfortunately, the officers, who had more room in the caboose, were in pitiful condition. One man's letter home describes what some of them suffered on that section of the route: "At one end of the car, lying on a stretcher on the floor was a poor fellow suffering from rheumatism and quite helpless with surgeon

Ryerson patiently sitting at his head where he had been trying all night, with little success, to snatch a little sleep. The gallant colonel … with elbows on knees, was sitting over the stove looking thoughtfully into the embers with eyes that have not known a wink of sleep for 50 hours. Then there was Major Dawson whose system appeared to be rebelling against the regularity of life to which it had been so long accustomed … Captain Harston, with a face as red as a boiled lobster sitting with arms folded on his knees [was] the very picture of incarnate discomfort"

On the map, Bandeville appeared as a town. But it actually consisted of a single shack in the wilderness. Here the men were given sandwiches and hot tea. Some were so stiff with cold they had to be lifted out of the cars. Others were so bone weary that the warmth of the shack was too much for them after the cold of the journey. They dropped off into a sleep so deep it was impossible to wake them.

Now the men prepared for the next leg of the journey – seven chilling hours before end of track at Port Munro was reached. Port Munro was a construction station and supply depot on the lakeshore, and here the troops were able to enjoy their first real sleep. In a deep, natural harbour, dominated by thousand-foot (300 m) crags, lay the schooner *Breck*. Two hundred troops slumbered aboard her, crowded together in the hold on mattresses composed of hay and dirt, and later of water. That leakage was caused by the weight of the human cargo grinding the vessel down through the ice. By the time the Halifax battalion arrived, the floor was afloat and pumps could not be worked because of the frost.

A second gap in the line, some twenty miles (32 km) long, began at Port Munro and continued to McKellar's Harbour, a small inlet near the mouth of the Little Pic River. There were not enough sleighs to carry more than the baggage, so the troops had to march across the glare ice of Lake Superior to the next piece of track. That journey took eight hours. They began in high spirits:

> The volunteers are all fine boys and full
> of lots of fun
> But it's mighty little pay they get for
> carrying a gun;
> The Government has grown so lean and the
> CPR so fat
> Our extra pay we did not get —
> You can bet your boots on that!

The Grenadiers, well fed and rested, moved out onto the ice at dawn on Easter Sunday – a long line of men with teams drawn up all around the bay. A black mountain towered above them, and the sun's first rays, red as blood, streamed down on the ice, lighting up the crags on the far side of the harbour. A bugle sounding the advance split the sharp morning air. When the men began to sing "Hold the

Fort for We Are Coming," the echoes of their voices bounded across the rocks.

When the column of men moved out into the cold bosom of the lake, the joy did not last long. For the very sun that had greeted them that morning was to prove the worst of enemies. The glare on the ice was bad, even for those who had been issued sunglasses. These men came in with their faces scorched and blistered, sometimes almost beyond recognition. Others made eye-coverings, Indian-fashion, out of strips of birchbark with thin slits cut into them. But others were rendered painfully blind – a red haze blotting out all vision, as if the eyes had been sandpapered. Colonel Otter himself, at the head of his troops, was almost totally blind when the end of track was reached.

Buffeted by piercing winds on one side and blistered by the sun's glare on the other, the troops were strung out for seven miles (11.2 km) across the lake. Marching was all but impossible because the surface was glassy. Then, after ten miles (16 km), the texture changed. Deep cuts, broken blocks of ice, and rocks frozen into the surface began to tear at the feet of the men, especially those who had left home in light shoes. Some threw their kits away, piece by piece. Some collapsed in their tracks. Some became temporarily crazy. One man was ruptured. The baggage sleighs followed behind to pick up the casualties.

The track across the lake was only nine inches (22.5 cm) wide. If a man slipped off it, he would plunge into snow six to eight feet (1.8 to 2.4 m) deep. The men couldn't stop for a moment for fear of being frozen, even though the sun was burning the skin off their faces.

It was bad enough by day – but the conditions at night were fearful. The men crossed the lake like sleepwalkers in the blackness. The freezing weather, accompanied by a heavy snowstorm with a wild piercing wind, made the march a frightening undertaking. Any man who drifted away from the column knew he faced almost certain death. To prevent that, guards were assigned to ride around to head off the drifters and stragglers. Even the guide appointed to lead the troops lost his way, lengthening the ordeal by several hours.

The cavalry were even worse off. The infantry marched across the ice as far as McKellar's Harbour, where a short piece of line had been laid to Jackfish Bay. But because of the nuisance of loading and unloading horses for such a short distance, the Governor-General's Body Guard decided to ride or walk their steeds the full thirty-five miles (56 km) to Jackfish over the ice of the lake.

After about fifteen miles (24 km), the baggage sleighs turned off to the right to proceed to the track. The cavalry men halted for lunch, drew their horses up in line, adjusted the nosebags, and then, standing in the lee of their mounts, munched on chunks of frozen bread, washed down with lake water drawn from a hole chopped in the ice.

The remainder of the trip was another nightmare. Up to this point, the track had been marked by the passage of sleigh runners. But now the men on horses were on their own. For the next twenty miles (32 km) they faced a vast desert of ice, with snow and drifts everywhere, and no track of any kind. The surface was obscured by a crust under which two or three inches (5 or 7.5 cm) of water lay concealed. Above that crust there was about as much as a foot (0.3 m) of light snow. This treacherous surface was broken by equally dangerous patches of glare ice. Through this chill morass, the horses, none of them with hind shoes, slipped, floundered, and struggled for mile after mile.

At the head of the column rode its commander, Lieutenant-Colonel George Taylor Denison III, a member of the most distinguished military family in Canada, an impressive figure – sabre straight, with bristling moustache, and firm features.

Denison quickly realized he was leading his men into a trap. They were miles from the shore in a wilderness of ice and snow-covered islands. It was clear a serious blizzard was about to descend upon them. Denison's idea was to move as swiftly as possible and get to land before the storm hit, but the ice was so bad the entire regiment came to a stop. Denison fanned his men out, seeking a route through the ice. When he found one, he rode on ahead with his adjutant, picking their way between the hummocks of land and ice. The first snowflakes were beginning to fall, but by good luck the blizzard held off until eight that evening when the cavalry finally reached Jackfish.

The York Rangers had an equally uncomfortable adventure. They crossed the same gap in a driving storm of rain and sleet, trudging up to their knees in a gruel of snow and water, in gutters eight inches (20 cm) deep left by the blades of the cutters.

At McKellar's Harbour, the men were forced to wait six hours for the flat cars to come back for them. The temperature dropped, and their soaking wet clothes began to freeze on their backs. They built roaring fires and clustered around them, scorching in front and freezing behind, until the train finally arrived.

These long waits without shelter were among the cruellest experiences on the route to the North West. The Queen's Own, for example, endured three of these waits – two hours in a blinding sleet storm when a train broke down at Carleton Place, nine hours in the freezing cold at McKellar's Harbour, and four hours in driving sleet at Winston's Dock. Most of these waiting periods were spent standing up. It was simply too cold and too wet to sit down.

The next gap began at Jackfish Bay. The soldiers, badly sunburned and frostbitten, with their faces masses of blisters and their feet bruised and swollen, were billeted in shanties, freight houses, and empty transport cars. Here was more hot food – blackstrap molasses, pork, potatoes, tea, and hard-tack. And then, for the lucky ones, a twenty-seven-mile (43.2 km) sleigh ride through the wet sleet to Winston's Dock. The rest faced a forced march through the heaped snow.

Now the bone-weary troops, gazing from the rims of the cutters and through the slats of the flat cars, began to see what Van Horne had faced. At Jackfish they could see the gaping mouth of one of the longest tunnels on the road, piercing a solid wall of rock, 150 feet (45 m) high, and stretching on for 500 feet (150 m). For nine miles (14.4 km) on end the roadbed had been blasted from the billion-year-old schists and granites of the Shield – chipped into the sheer surface of the dark cliffs or hacked right through the spiny ridges by means of deep cuts. In some places it seemed as if the whole side of a mountain had been ripped apart by dynamite and hurled into the deep, still waters of the lake.

The voyage between Winston's Dock and Nepigon was again made on rails that had been laid directly over the snow. Here the scenery grew grander. As the cars crawled along, the soldiers began to stand up in the seats to see sights they would never forget – the road torn out of the solid rock for mile after mile, skirting the very edge of the lake, from whose shores the mountains rose up directly. On some of the cars the soldiers produced songbooks and began to sing.

Did any of them consider, during these brief moments of relaxation, the high cost of being Canadian? Did any of them pause to question the necessity of shipping them all off on a partly finished railroad on a bleak and friendless land? Did any of them measure the price to be paid in loss of national dignity against the easier passage through the United States? Did any of them think that it could have been accomplished just as quickly, and no more awkwardly and with a lot less physical suffering? But there's no evidence that anyone – soldier, general, politician, or journalist – ever seriously considered that alternative.

There was one final gap to come. For many it would be the most terrible of all. This was a short march over the ice of the lake between Nepigon and Red Rock. It was only ten miles (16 km), but it took some troops as long as six hours to do it.

The 10th Grenadiers started out in the evening into the darkness of the pines and hemlocks, along a trail so narrow that any attempt to move in columns of four had to be scrapped. It was almost impossible to stay on the track. And yet one misstep caused a man to be buried to his neck in deep snow.

They emerged from the woods and onto the ice of the lake – "the worst ice that ever mortal man encountered" – and were met by a pitiless, pelting rain that seemed to drive through the thickest clothing. The rain had softened the track made by the sleighs, covering it with a slush so deep that every step a man took brought him into six inches of icy porridge.

All attempts to preserve distance under such conditions had to be abandoned. The officers and men were forced to link arms to prevent tumbling. To move through the slush they had to raise their knees almost to their waists, as if marking time – a strenuous, exhausting effort because, in effect, they waded the entire distance.

Slogging through the slush of Lake Superior country.

As the rain increased, the lights of Red Rock, beckoning in the distance, winked out behind a wall of water. Now and then a man would tumble exhausted into the slush and lie unnoticed until somebody stumbled over him. One officer counted some forty men lying in the snow in this way, many of them face down, completely played out.

Some actually fell asleep as they marched. Others fell by the wayside and couldn't speak. A member of the York Rangers described one such case: "On the way across one of the boys of the 35th was so fagged out that he laid down on the sleigh and could not move an inch. Captain Thomson asked him to move to one side but not one inch would he stir, so he caught hold of him like bag and baggage, and tossed him to one side to let him pass."

By the time they reached Red Rock, the men were like zombies. They stood in ankle-deep ice water waiting for the trains, not knowing where they were. When the trains arrived, they tumbled into the cars and dropped in their tracks, lying on the floor, twisted on the seats all of a heap, sleeping where they fell.

One man, the son of a British general, crumpled up onto the floor in such a position that his head was under the seat "and no amount of shaking would wake him to improve his situation." There was tea ready for them all but, cold and wet as they were, many did not have the strength to drink it.

The ordeal was at an end. The track, as they well knew, now lay unbroken to their destination at Qu'Appelle.

There would be no marching until the coulées of Saskatchewan were reached – time enough to reckon with Dumont's sharpshooters. For the moment, at least, they had no worries, and so, like men already dead, they slept.

CHAPTER NINE

The eleventh hour

THE NATIVE PEOPLES OF THE PLAINS MADE their final, futile gesture against the onrushing tidal wave of civilization in the deep coulées of the north Saskatchewan country in May and June. The impetuous Gabriel Dumont, restrained only by a leader who had become increasingly mystical and irrational, finally broke away and met the militia at Fish Creek. Here the young men who had endured the trials of the Canadian Shield were lured into a kind of buffalo pound, where Dumont vowed to treat them exactly as he had the thundering herds in the brave days before the railway.

There his force of 130 Métis, armed for the most part with ancient shotguns and muzzle loaders, held back some 800 trained men under General Middleton, the bumbling and over-cautious British Army regular. Then, on May 2 at Cut Knife Hill, Chief Poundmaker and 325 Cree followers emerged victorious against cannon, Gatling gun, and Colonel Otter's 540 troops.

But these were the last contortions of a dying culture. The Canadian government had 8,000 men in the field, transported and supplied by the new railway. The Indians had fewer than 1,000 under arms, and these were neither organized nor, in all cases, enthusiastic. Riel planned his campaign according to the almost daily spiritual visits he believed he received.

The more practical and pugnacious Dumont used his knowledge of the ground, his skill at swift manoeuvre and deception, and his experience in the organization of the great buffalo hunts to fend off superior forces. Perhaps if Riel had given him his head, he might have cut the main CPR line, derailed the trains, and harried the troops for months in a running guerrilla warfare. That would have stopped western settlement for years. But the outcome would have been the same.

In mid-May, Dumont fought his last battle at Batoche. It lasted for four days, until his ammunition ran out. It was remarkable, among other things, for the use of the first and only prairie warship. It also brought Riel's surrender and the flight of Dumont, who subsequently re-enacted the incidents of 1885 in Buffalo Bill's Wild West Show.

The rebellion had wrenched the gaze of settled Canada out to the prairie country and focused it on the railway. Every major newspaper had a war correspondent who travelled with the troops, reporting on their condition and the hardships they faced. But with these dispatches came something else – a new awareness of the land and of the railway's relation to it.

Thanks to Van Horne there were comments on the thoughtfulness and courtesy of their CPR attendants and amazement at the engineering marvels he had worked along the lakeshore. Week after week Canadians were treated to a continuing geography lesson about a land that some had scarcely considered part of the nation. Until 1885, it had been as a foreign country. Now their boys were fighting in it and for it, and soon anyone who wanted to see it could do so for the price of a railway ticket.

The CPR, meanwhile, was teetering on the edge of financial bankruptcy. But as Joseph Henry Pope, the minister of railways, told John A. Macdonald, if the railway went bankrupt, the government could not survive. The mood of the country was beginning to change. Because of the swift action of the railway, the government had a good chance of controlling the Saskatchewan Rebellion and preventing it from spreading.

Finally, after a long debate in Parliament – it lasted for the best part of a month – the bill to relieve the CPR with government loan guarantees was passed. It came July 10, and not a moment too soon, for the company's credit had reached the breaking point. With a line across the Shield now complete and only a few dozen miles remaining to be filled in in the mountains, the railway was saved at the eleventh hour. It is doubtful if history records another instance of a national enterprise coming so close to ruin and surviving.

Before the end of the year, Riel was dead – hanged at Regina – and Canada was joined by a line of steel from sea to sea.

Index